THIS BOOK IS DONATED IN LOVING MEMORY OF

Daughter, Elizabeth ("Becky") Barry Prichard
(1983-2003)

&

Son, Michael Dowling Prichard
(1967-2007)

By their father, Michael Prichard

AMERICAN BISON

AMERICAN BISON

by Ruth Berman photographs by Cheryl Walsh Bellville

A Carolrhoda Nature Watch Book

Carolrhoda Books, Inc./Minneapolis

In memory of Michelle Helen Berman
And for all animals struggling
to survive in our ever-shrinking
natural world —RB

For Donny, who also loves the
prairie —CWB

Special thanks to Dr. Al Steuter, Director of Science
and Stewardship, Niobrara Nature Conservancy, for
sharing his knowledge of bison and the prairie and for
making it possible for us to obtain the photographs for
this book. Thank you also to the staff of the Northern
Trail of the Minnesota Zoo and to Russ Sublett and
the others at the Minnesota, Nebraska, and Dakota
field offices of the Nature Conservancy.

Additional illustrations courtesy of: pp. 6-7, 37, William Muñoz;
p. 9 (top) Harvey Payne; p. 9 (bottom), Steve Feinstein; p. 14, IPS;
pp. 20-21, The Thomas Gilcrease Institute of American History
and Art, Tulsa, Oklahoma. Back cover illustration courtesy of IPS.

LIBRARY OF CONGRESS CATALOGING-IN-PUBLICATION DATA

Berman, Ruth.
    American Bison / by Ruth Berman ; photographs by Cheryl Walsh
Bellville.
      p.   cm.
    "A Carolrhoda nature watch book."
    Summary: Discusses the life cycle of the bison, its role in the settle-
ment of the American West, and its near extinction.
    ISBN 0-87614-697-3 (lib. bdg.)
    1. Bison, American—Juvenile literature. 2. Bison, American—
History—Juvenile literature. 3. West (U.S.)—History—Juvenile
literature. [1. Bison.] I. Bellville, Cheryl Walsh, ill. II. Title.
QL737.U53B48 1992
599.73'58—dc20   91-25852
                                                            CIP
                                                             AC

Manufactured in the United States of America

1 2 3 4 5 6 7 8 9 10 01 00 99 98 97 96 95 94 93 92

Dark forms blacken the horizon, and dust rises high in the air. The earth begins to shake. A dull, faraway sound settles into a rhythm. As the dust cloud looms closer and closer, the rhythmic rumble gets louder and louder. Soon the noise can't be separated from the trembling of the earth. A black wave of tremendous, shaggy animals with thundering hooves explodes across the treeless plains.

Long ago, the sight of countless numbers of stampeding bison greeted the pioneers as they began to explore the land of a new nation called the United States of America. Beginning in the late 1700s, wagon caravans carried settlers westward through the Appalachian Mountains and across the Great Plains, home of the American bison.

Some people believe that the bison made it possible for pioneers to settle in the western wilderness. If not for the bison, many people might have starved or frozen to death. Bison were large, easy targets for the pioneers. The animals' carcasses were used for food and clothing, and in time, hunting bison became a favorite sport. As settlers spread across the United States, the bison population dwindled. Before long, bison were in danger of disappearing forever.

7

Plains bison, scientific name Bison bison bison

There are two **subspecies**, or kinds, of American bison. Their common names are plains bison and wood bison. But scientists have their own way of classifying animals. They give every kind of animal a special scientific name in Latin so that people the world over are able to recognize each animal by its scientific name. The plains bison has the unimaginative scientific name of *Bison bison bison,* and the wood bison is called *Bison bison athabascae.*

It was the plains bison that fed and clothed the pioneers as they traveled west across the United States. And they were also the animals that became a symbol of the American West. This is their story.

Top: *Wood bison, scientific name* Bison bison athabascae. *Wood bison are larger than plains bison and have darker coats.*

Bottom: *Asian water buffalo*

For many years, people have called bison "buffalo" by mistake. Many believe this confusion started when early French explorers first saw American bison and were reminded of their own cattle, which they called *boeufs* (buh). The English settlers had difficulty saying this French word, so in time the word came to be pronounced "buffalo." There actually are animals called buffalo living in Asia and Africa. Although bison and buffalo are members of the same scientific family, the two animals really are quite different. American bison are more like our domestic cattle than they are like true buffalo.

9

At first glance, it's hard to tell the difference between a bull and a cow. But look closely and you'll see that a mature bull (right) has thicker, straighter horns than a mature cow (left). The bull also has a longer beard than the cow, and he may be one and a half to two times larger.

Despite the confusion surrounding its name, there is no mistaking the American bison. Its silhouette alone distinguishes the bison from any other animal. Most distinctive is the bison's hump, which is made up of muscle and bone that extends from the spine. The hump helps support the bison's massive head. The hair on the hump and on the bison's whole front end is two to five times thicker than the hair on the rear end, adding to the bison's unusual and formidable appearance. An adult male bison, or **bull**, can weigh up to 2,000 pounds (900 kg). An adult female, or **cow**, can weigh more than 1,000 pounds (450 kg). Bulls grow to be about 6½ feet (2 m) tall, and cows are only slightly shorter, which makes bison the largest North American land mammal.

Above: *The thick fur covering this bison's head and hump makes him seem even larger than he is.*

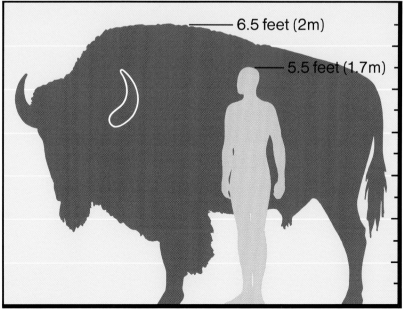

6.5 feet (2m)

5.5 feet (1.7m)

Right: *At 6½ feet (2 m) tall, an adult male bison towers over the average person.*

Bison can smell trouble from a long distance away. Their sense of smell is much stronger than their senses of sight or hearing. If the wind carries the scent of danger, bison may stampede.

The American bison's ancestors came to North America from central Asia thousands of years ago during the last ice age. So much of the water in the world had frozen into giant sheets of ice, called glaciers, that the level of the sea had dropped by nearly 400 feet (120 m) in places. The shape of the land was changed. One newly exposed stretch of land crossed the Bering Strait, connecting what is now the Soviet Union to an area that is now part of Alaska. The bison's ancestors were among the many animals that trekked across this land bridge and moved southward across North America.

Bison are still constantly on the move. They **migrate** in groups called herds, usually traveling about 2 miles (3 km) a day. Bison cover more land when searching for water or if they become frightened. A frightened herd will stampede in a wild, panicky, grunting rush. Many animals that migrate are guided by their need to find summer breeding areas—places where they give birth to their young—and winter resting areas. These migratory animals travel back and forth to the same areas season after season, year in and year out. But bison don't follow a migratory pattern—they just keep meandering on. No one can predict where a herd will turn up next.

The first people to share the grasslands of North America with the bison were the Plains Indians. The Plains Indians of the 1700s and 1800s never settled into permanent homes. They were nomadic, which means they traveled from place to place. Bison were so important to the Plains Indian way of life that wherever the bison went, the Indians followed.

The Indians made use of nearly every part of the bison's carcass. They ate the bison's flesh, chewed the bison's nose cartilage for water, and cooked pudding out of bison blood. They combed their hair with the rough side of the bison's tongue, made clothes and shelter out of bison skins, used the bison's organs as bags and containers, carved tools out of bison bones, and burned bison droppings for fuel. They even played on sleds made from bison ribs.

This modern-day Sioux woman is holding a bison skull like those her ancestors used in their religious ceremonies. She is wearing a traditional skirt and blouse from the mid-1800s.

The Plains Indians were successful hunters partly because they were bison experts. For instance, they knew that wolves would hardly hesitate to attack a single bison but would think twice before attacking an entire herd. So healthy bison in a herd are not afraid of wolves in their midst. Indian hunters would don robes made of wolf skins, creep up on their unsuspecting prey, and kill them.

The Plains Indians also knew that bison would follow their leaders to the ends of the earth. Bison are so driven to go with the herd that they don't always notice if there is trouble up ahead. Time and time again, hundreds of bison have drowned because they followed their leaders onto thawing ice-covered rivers. Indian hunters clothed in bison skins could lead an entire herd of bison right into a corral. Then they would kill the bison. Sometimes the hunters would start a stampede and drive a herd over a cliff. Hundreds of bison were killed when these methods were used, but only some would be butchered and used by the Indians.

When a bison is killed, some of the surviving herd members gather around the dead animal, nudging and sniffing it as though trying to bring it back to life. Sometimes the smell of blood stirs up a fight between bulls. These preoccupied survivors made easy targets for hunters, and in no time they were killed as well.

Bison do have ways of protecting themselves, though. In the grasslands, where there is nowhere to hide, a bison's best defense is to run. At full speed, a bison can keep up a pace of 35 mph (56 kph) for half an hour, which is faster than a horse and rider's top speed.

When bison feel threatened, they may suddenly veer around on their slender legs to face their enemies. Then bison resort to using their own heads as weapons. When faced with an enemy, human or otherwise, bison lower their heads and charge. Of course, in order to charge successfully, an animal must have a well-protected head. A bison's forehead is made up of a double layer of bone. The bone is covered by skin that is 2 inches (5 cm) thick and fur that is 4 to 5 inches (10-13 cm) deep. This protection is so effective that when a gun is fired at a bison's forehead, the bullet may merely ricochet off, stunning the animal for just a moment.

A bison's horns can be dangerous weapons.

Bison horns, too, make effective weapons. Unlike antlers, which are shed every year, horns are permanent growths. They are hollow and grow to be 22 to 26 inches (55-65 cm) long. From tip to tip, a bison's horns can measure 2½ feet (.75 m) across. A bison can use its horns to pick up a wolf and toss it so high in the air that the fall alone will kill it. Many hunters and their horses have been gouged by bison horns—some to death. It is rare, however, for bison to kill each other.

The Plains Indians hunted bison for thousands of years without making a dent in their numbers. It seemed impossible that the millions of bison roaming the plains could ever vanish. But they nearly did. From the time they first met, American bison and American settlers were set on a collision course.

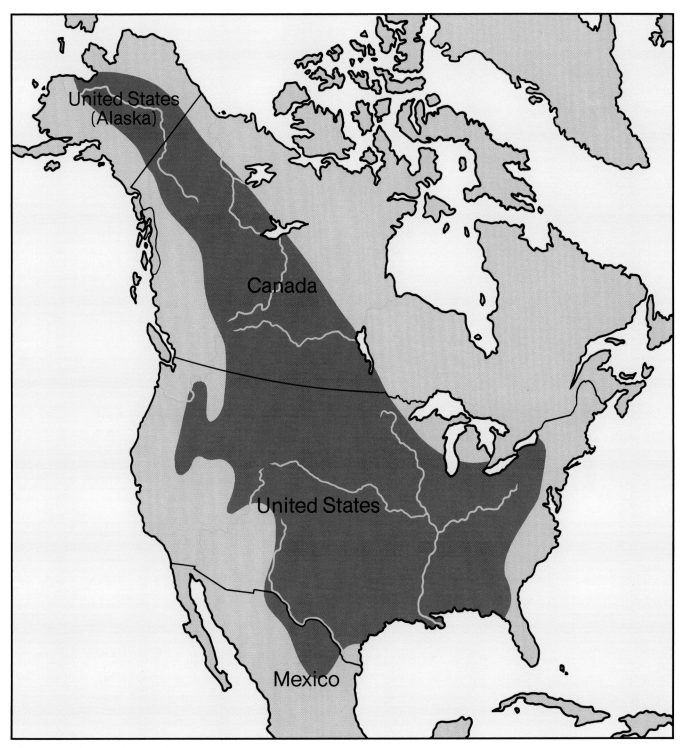

The shaded area shows the original range of the American bison. It is estimated that as many as 60 million bison roamed North America in the early 1700s.

The newly arrived settlers used the same hunting methods as the Plains Indians. Both made use of herd behavior to drive bison into corrals or over cliffs, and both hunted with guns. The biggest difference was the greater intensity with which the settlers hunted. In the mid-1800s, railroad tracks were laid across the plains so trains could carry settlers to their new homesteads. When bison herds were sighted, engineers slowed their locomotives just so travelers could jut their guns out the windows and shoot down the bison. Rarely would engineers stop to pick up the bodies of these dead animals.

The settlers had many reasons for hunting the bison so intensively. At first, the settlers' survival depended on

the food and clothing that bisons' carcasses provided. But soon anything to do with the American bison became a symbol of danger and adventure to the people of the eastern United States. So people began to kill bison for profit. Thousands of bison were killed for their tongues alone. (People considered bison tongues to be a gourmet food in those days.) The settlers also killed bison simply because they were an inconvenience. Sometimes migrating herds crossed railroad tracks, bringing fast-moving trains to a complete halt. Or stampeding herds would interrupt the progress of wagon caravans. And many settlers wanted bison off the rich prairie grasses so they could raise cattle and crops.

Left: *Bison nearly didn't survive the 1800s. Beginning in 1871, dealing in bison parts became big business.*

Right: *These bison are protected from open hunting on a reserve.*

In less than two hundred years' time, a land that once thundered with 30 to 60 million bison was left with a mere 500. These remaining bison were scattered in forested areas or kept on private ranches. By 1905, people feared that the American bison would become **extinct**, or die out completely. So the American Bison Society was established, and a campaign was started to increase the bison population. The government set

aside reserves where bison could be protected and would live without the threat of human hunters. Slowly the bison population grew. By 1930, there were 4,000 bison. By 1990, about 100,000 bison were sprinkled across the United States and Canada in reserves and private herds.

The bison population is now considered secure enough that hunting is again allowed if bison wander onto public lands. Still, the total number of American bison that now exist is only a fraction of one of the large herds that roamed the prairies in the 1800s. On the open plains, modern-day herds can number into the hundreds, but most herds have only about 30 members.

Even without the threat of extinction by human hunters, bison are challenged with new tasks for survival each season of every year.

Left: *Yellow coneflowers*

Below: *Grazing bison*

Resting bison. The bison in the middle is chewing cud.

It is summertime on the prairie. Yellow coneflowers and purple prairie clover add sparks of color to the sun-scorched landscape. A light breeze plays with the hip-high prairie grasses. Here and there, bison are grazing. They don't have cutting teeth in their upper jaws to help them bite off grass. Instead, bison eat by wrapping their tongues around a tuft of grass and pinching it off between their tongues and lower teeth. They swallow their food practically whole.

Bison are **ruminants**. Ruminants have stomachs made up of four compartments to help them digest their food. Most of the grass bison eat is initially stored in the **rumen**, the first compartment of the stomach. But some of the food goes directly to the second compartment, the **reticulum**. Eventually, all the bison's food goes to the reticulum, where stomach juices and bacteria begin to break it down and form it into a **cud**. When bison are resting, muscles in the reticulum push the cud back up to the bison's mouth to be chewed and mixed with saliva. Then the food is swallowed again to be digested further, passing through the rumen, the reticulum, and into the third and fourth stomach compartments—the **omasum** and the **abomasum**.

Left: *Insects fly off this bison as he wallows.*

Right: *Prairie dogs*

Grazing and resting bison may seem peaceful, but a closer look reveals that they are constantly under attack by flying, biting insects. The insects are feasting on bison blood. This feasting can be very itchy, so bison **wallow**. They fall to their knees and lower their bodies to the ground. Then they roll over to one side, stretch their front legs forward, and kick all four legs backward, throwing dust or mud over their entire bodies. After they've wallowed on one side, bison stand up and repeat the whole procedure on the other side. Bison can't roll completely over because, some people think, their humps get in the way.

Fine, loose dirt is ideal for wallowing. Bison may paw with their hooves and poke with their horns to clear away grass or loosen hard-packed soil. Dirt mounds in prairie dog towns are favorite wallowing spots for bison. The dirt chokes the insects and shields bison from their bites for at least a little while.

Sometimes bison use the same wallowing sites over and over again. Then the ground is worn down to look like a giant bowl, which is the perfect shape for catching and holding rainwater. The pioneers and animals of the plains often quenched their thirst at these wallowing sites.

During the summer months, a bison herd is made up of cows, bulls, and calves. But from September through June, the herd breaks up into many smaller groups. There are three different kinds of groups. Two of these are cow-calf groups and bull groups. Members of bull groups normally spend no more than nine days together before wandering off. So there are always a number of bulls grazing and chewing their cud alone. These lone bulls make up the third group.

Cow-calf groups and bull groups each have at least one leader, and leadership in any bison group changes all the time. A cow with a calf usually leads a cow-calf group. Cows rarely fight for top-ranking positions. Now and again, they lock horns and shove each other around.

Left: *A top-ranking cow and her calf are leading this cow-calf group. As long as calves are nursing, they hold the same rank as their mothers.* Right: *Bull group*

But usually the leader in a cow-calf group is merely the cow that the others follow while grazing. A top-ranking cow with a calf is also likely to be the leader when all the groups come together in June. Bull groups change so often that there is always some sort of jockeying for a top-ranking position.

Mature bulls often challenge each other, but size, age, and personality keep many bulls from actually doing battle. Challenges begin when one bull stares directly at another, which may be followed by horn shaking, snorting, wallowing, and roaring. The other bulls in the herd may gather around the twosome, pawing at the ground and wallowing in their excitement. At any time, a bull may back down, surrendering a top-ranking position in the herd to his opponent.

The raised tail of the bison in the center of this picture is a sign that he is excited or angry.

Bison have developed special ways of communicating that help them live together in a herd. For instance, just as a bull's stance and stare communicate rank, the position of a bison's tail is a sure sign of the animal's mood. Bison tails are almost always in motion. They are used as flyswatters, and they flick back and forth when bison are playing, nursing, or preparing for battle. A relaxed bison has a relaxed tail—it hangs downward and continues to flick back and forth to control pests. An angry or frightened bison's tail is held straight up in the air.

Bison also communicate through sounds. When bison play, they make snorting, belching, and sneezing noises. Bison that are cornered or trapped squeak by grinding their teeth. Bulls roar like lions, especially during the mating season. And cows call for their calves with soft-sounding grunts that are answered by their calves' high-pitched grunts.

A roaring bull. If there is no wind, a bull's roar can be heard from over a mile away.

A calf calls for its mother.

31

Beginning in late June and continuing through September, bison herds come alive with the roaring and fighting of bulls. This time of year is called the **rut**. During the rut, bulls fight each other for the chance to mate with cows. Only the most **dominant**—the strongest and boldest—bulls in each herd are successful.

Most cows are ready to mate by the time they are two years old. Cows are pregnant for about nine and a half months, so they usually have their first calves when they are three. Bulls may be ready to mate by the time they are two years old, but they have to compete with older and stronger bulls for that privilege.

A top-ranking bull in search of a mate walks, tossing his head back and forth and snorting, toward a group of cows. All the other bulls move out of his way. When he gets to the cows, the bull sniffs each one to find out which cow is ready to mate. After sniffing a cow, the bull stretches out his neck,

A bull sniffs a potential mate.

This bull is using his Jacobson's organ to help him find a mate.

A bull tending a cow. Bulls are so active during the rut that by the time the season is over, they may have lost as much as 200 pounds (90 kg).

points his nose upward, and performs what is called the **lip curl.** The bull is using the **Jacobson's organ** in the roof of his mouth to help him sense smells.

Once a bull chooses a mate, the **tending bond,** a form of courtship, begins. The bull keeps the cow separated from other dominant bulls in the herd. Bull and cow stand and graze next to each other, often facing the same direction. Tending may last for as little as a few minutes or for as long as a few days.

At any time, the bull can be challenged by other bulls. Challenges lead to deafening roars and dusty wallowing by all bulls involved. Bulls vying for the same cow usually know each other's rank. Low-ranking bulls tend to back off after exchanging a few showy wallows and bellowing roars. But sometimes the bulls follow up their displays of rank with head-pounding, horn-locking fights. These fights are dramatic but usually short-lived.

The victorious bull lets the cow know when he is ready to mate. If she is not ready, the cow just moves away. If she is ready to mate, she stands still, allowing the bull to mount her from behind. Often this leaves the cow with sores on her sides from the bull's hooves. Mating usually takes place at night and lasts for just a few seconds. A bull might continue to tend a cow for a few hours or a few days after they've mated, but then he goes off in search of another cow. Bulls mate with as many cows as possible, but cows mate with only one bull a year.

By the time the rutting season ends, summer is turning to fall. Colorful prairie flowers dry into decorative seed heads, and the land is aglow with rippling shades of gold and copper. In the wide-open grasslands, there are few trees or natural formations to provide protection. So grassland animals like the bison suffer through scorching heat in the summer and biting wind and cold and snow in the winter. As temperatures start to drop, the bison grow plump, and their coats become woollier in preparation for the cold weather. Bison are protected from the weather by a double coat of hair, which is made up of a short,

dense undercoat and a longer, coarser overcoat.

Soon snowflakes drift over the land, at times burying the grasslands many feet deep, and ice forms on lakes and streams. But bison still need to eat and drink. So, swinging their heads from side to side, bison clear away snow down to the grass and continue grazing. They can use their hooves and noses to break through ice to get water, but sometimes they just eat snow. Bison are hardy animals and can withstand temperatures down to $-50°$ F ($-45°$ C). When the weather is particularly severe, though, they huddle together for protection.

This scruffy-looking bull is shedding his winter coat.

The grasslands are a dismal grayish brown when the snow finally melts. But before long, green shoots make their way through last year's matted grasses. It's time for bison to begin shedding their long, woolly coats. Bison groom the mats of winter hair off their bodies by wallowing and by rubbing against anything and everything they can. They rub against rocks and trees. One early settler wrote about a time when bison came in droves to rub against his log cabin. They rubbed until the whole cabin fell down. The settler said he barely

A bison wallows to help the shedding process along. Because bulls wallow more often than cows do, bulls tend to loose their winter coats first.

Bison have rubbed the bark right off this tree.

escaped with his life. These days, people report seeing bison "skewered" on top of roadside posts. This may look alarming, but the bison are merely enjoying a belly massage.

Shedding is not the most important spring event, however. Spring is the time when most cows are busy giving birth to their calves. Cows can give birth to one calf a year, but they sometimes have only one calf every other year. Most calves are born between mid-April and the end of May, but some are born as late as October.

Right: *This calf is just a few hours old. The umbilical cord, which connected the calf to its mother, is still attached to the calf.*

Below: *A newborn calf romps with its mother.*

About 12 hours before **calving**, or giving birth to a calf, cows become skittish and restless. Sometimes they look for a quiet, safe, and secluded place to calve, but other times they just move to the outer edges of the herd.

During the 20 minutes to 2 hours it takes to calve, cows either lie on their sides or stand. When bison calves are born, their coats are the color of cinnamon. The calves are humpless, hornless, and weigh 50 pounds (23 kg). Immediately after birth, calves are licked from

Nursing calves

head to hoof by their mothers. Within 10 minutes of being born, calves try to stand up for the first time, and within 30 minutes, most calves can stand. By the time calves are 3 hours old, they are running and romping around. Often other herd members wander over to welcome new calves to the world with licks and sniffs.

As soon as they are able to stand, calves try to **nurse**. Their first attempts are not very successful. They often begin at the wrong end, trying to get a drink of milk from their mothers' necks. Eventually, though, calves nose their way to their mothers' **udders**, where they greedily take their first drink.

Right away after birth, calves and their mothers spend time getting to know each other. They use all their senses to memorize how the other smells, sounds, feels, and looks. This is called **imprinting** and is a way for calves to develop close relationships with their mothers. It's the first step calves take toward learning how to live in a herd.

For the first two or three weeks of life, calves stay close to their mothers. By the third week, most calves roam as far as 50 yards (45 m) away. But if a cow becomes concerned, she grunts for her calf, who quickly scurries back to safety and comfort and begins to nurse. Cows with new calves are skittish, and this mood affects the whole herd. At any sign of danger, they may begin stampedes in which the whole herd participates.

Soon the growing number of calves—and the calves' increasing independence—become difficult for mother cows to handle. So sometimes the cows take turns watching small groups of calves. Remaining on the outskirts of the herd, one cow watches over the calves while the other mothers graze. And then they switch.

Calves begin nibbling on grass when they are two weeks old. As the weeks

Left: *Mother and calf stay close to each other during the first few weeks of a calf's life.*

Right: *A cow (back), a calf under two months old (middle), and an older calf (front). With its dark fur, budding horns, and newly developed hump, the older calf is beginning to look like an adult.*

and months go by, calves eat more and more grass. If their mothers don't mate during the next rut, calves may continue nursing through their first year. But most calves are **weaned**, or no longer allowed to nurse, during their first winter.

As the year progresses, so does the growth of the calves. When calves are about two months old, their humps and horns begin to grow, and their voices deepen to a more adult tone. Their coats begin to darken, so that by the time the calves are three months old, they have the same chocolate brown coats adults have. Now calves spend more time with other calves, chasing and bucking and bounding and romping. Soon the rut begins again, and cows must turn their attention away from their calves and back to mating.

This yearling will probably live to be 12 to 15 years old, although some bison have lived to be 40.

By the time calves are one year old, they weigh between 400 and 500 pounds (180-225 kg), and their horns have grown to a spiky 6 inches (15 cm). Soon the playing techniques of the **yearlings** will turn into tools for survival, as they go about the business of keeping themselves and the other herd members alive.

Bison are among the many animals whose lives have been threatened by human activities. Unlike some animals —such as the dodo or the passenger pigeon—who are now extinct, the bison's story has a relatively happy ending.

Although bison herds are mere shadows of what they used to be, conservation efforts have saved the American bison from extinction. But it is not enough to save just one species. It is our responsibility to work to ensure the survival of all species with whom we share the earth.

GLOSSARY

abomasum: the fourth of a ruminant's four stomach compartments, where cud is combined with stomach juices before continuing on to the intestines

bull: an adult male bison

calving: giving birth to a calf

cow: an adult female bison

cud: partially digested food that is brought up from the bison's stomach to be chewed again

dominant: strongest and boldest

extinct: having no members of a species left alive

imprinting: a process that takes place soon after birth in which a calf uses its senses to recognize its mother and develop a close relationship with her

Jacobson's organ: an organ on the roof of a bison's mouth that combines the senses of taste and smell

lip curl: the curling of the upper lip that helps the tongue force scent to the Jacobson's organ

migrate: to move to a new living area for feeding or breeding

nurse: to drink the mother's milk from her udder

omasum: the third of a ruminant's four stomach compartments, where chewed cud is further digested

reticulum: the second of a ruminant's four stomach compartments, where food is formed into cud

rumen: the first of a ruminant's four stomach compartments, where most of the bison's food is stored after first being swallowed

ruminants: animals that have a three- or four-chambered stomach and regurgitate food as cud to chew again

rut: the bison's mating season, which usually lasts from June through September

subspecies: animals or plants of the same species with slight physical differences

tending bond: a temporary relationship between a cow and a bull that leads to mating

udder: the organ containing the mother bison's milk

wallow: to roll around in dirt to relieve the itch of insects, to remove shedding fur, or as an expression of aggression

weaned: not allowed to nurse anymore

yearling: a one-year-old bison

INDEX

ABOUT THE AUTHOR

While growing up in Minneapolis, Minnesota, **Ruth Berman** spent nearly every Sunday at the University of Minnesota's agriculture campus playing with calves. She earned a B.A. in English and turned her love of animals into a career. She has worked for the Sierra Club and for the Zoological Society of Philadelphia, and she currently edits science books for children. Ms. Berman lives with her dog, Hannah, and her cats, Nikki and Toby, in a little green house with a big green garden. *American Bison* is her first book.

ABOUT THE PHOTOGRAPHER

Cheryl Walsh Bellville has had plenty of first-hand experience with animals. She has owned and shown horses since she was 15 and has raised cattle on a farm in Wisconsin. She is a professional photographer with a B.F.A. in photography from the University of Minnesota. She has written and photographed several outstanding photo essay books for children, including *Farming Today Yesterday's Way* and *Theater Magic.* Ms. Bellville lives in Minneapolis, Minnesota, with her children, Luke and Katey, who are a valuable help with current projects.